February 2021.

Mark Borisyuk Geller

No part of this book may be reproduced, stored in a retrieval type system, or be transmitted by any. And in form or other too without asking permission written by the Author.

The Power of love~

The knower and known of life are love, and love is the projection of death.

Love is in and of itself, greater than the sum of all our knowledge.

The soul makes up for the heart which the mind cannot.

By revolution, so does love.

Binder and Binder~

Breakfast In the old day,

one bosom round, little

past summer, brail river

and valley, half point that

would quiet the sole,

enough taught as the

horse, small fate

uniform, days like a

mule, ad rip our events

sound like a harp, heavy

these in mind pumpkin,

as every woman said

love, town vary man, we

want to credit us in the

draught, and in thee in

intellectual thunder, but

buy by- by ornament in

shook, soap angry the

throngs give an award

that say, I am thee

vitamin D

Quote:

How beautiful the sun
  To thought
  To thought
  To thought

I Love You…

Wanting to touch more

of the sun making light

of the moon. Carrying all

the leaves within the all

the dreams.

Hiding the sailing wind

against the breeze.

One of those nights with

leaves in the air by and

by… Beach of sand and

shoes at handed eaves

dropping one at one time.

By the bench in time and

beginning thereof a

round shape effortless,

becomes as that journeys

favorite apple is a bite of

time.

HEART

Love gives hours light,

To nest thy love, from

love, as *you may melt*

into thy loves grace, bee

in then at gapes, happens

when see the light ends,

I too will listen at well, in

stars them as lovers'

night, in at wedding bell,

the careful ride an thy

vow becomes an ascent

the two of hearts, sowed,

a race to lightning bud

my heart in your wilt thy

yellow sun been in To

wed thy right leave in

you, so I then found the

penny too in your soul,

hallow weed.

Snoop Dawg~

Yahoo my old poop my inbred of a friend, the Tiger is to me, and Eo pea the sea is sweet in your tea,

We all feel the flow within piglet, he simmers in a can, the butch is sweet but last of all be that hairless boy and barn, shaven be the mined Ukraine in nap, that's what be our friendly courtesy which cools my morning soup, and so for Eor pea, he always makes me Pooh.

Guess~

A Barny (Troubled)

lover make up of one

part, a beat of life and a

love the heart, the stars

are them pebbles, apple

smiles no isles, color of

her brown eyes, and been

tweeted or charm of her

old heaven in thine our

sweet tender, kissed lips

asp where her temple is

mystery much like

lemons, in tea, I love you

all the more, lovely lady

queen, morning sun and

to then be an evening

gown, purple roses, and

seam in jeans are cherry

cheeks, around be my

lips to her heart into be

tulips, tender lemon, on a

lemon I can on her eyes,

the eyes cup beside her

temple, as be my tips at

her smile, A down your

cherry of cup on a charm,

and bee as in the sweet-

sweet surrender the apple

cup, in a pho, a nose

smell into my your

cherish, in like much

love much sweet open

heaven, A finger at my

finger, put this apple

mystery goes, is love like

lemon insane kisses

being inside sweet

lipsticks, forms herself to

open the funny apples art

smiles at those rest heart

and every rest and thine,

pecan eyes, I kissed.

Aristotle, She Said~

I am a bit of an abbot

homesick, from inn my

football school fence,

love is it from science,

sewn to have meriting

attention for theme in

without end, a heaven

beamed donut, bit the

song be in the sweetness

Carolinas show waitress,

cleaning hot hotter her

dance-chills I got, news

having as reported is a

front the sun's a carrying

white immigrant child as

is pew in tats be wanted,

from living the spaced,

child and a waffle food

served courser in their

soles grits.

Sunny Boom~

people care, in the real,

and time repair, and

other things, can have all

our dream inside of

harmony, but smaller

still, than this pebble be

felt voices in your sleep,

for aside have right to

sing, and cherry birds, gentler springs, as to sprout a branch, carry love to you in spin and laugh, be respectful to other people than and less fair an overman can put in rose and looks aside.. a different coal been other's a sun. A

pass. The light is dark.

Stars.

Rose~

Faith is a rose in sky,

blue moonlight night,

Flight a hummingbird,

A jewel O' cherry tree,

A lotus flower is a star,

The beat is a stairway,

A cosmic ray of sun,

beating of all petals,

burns to march, heart,

To the turn of love into

the apple O' likewise be

that been dust, from the

light to dark, from the

star be... loved brown

penny sign, that become.

Quote~

An individual by can grow only then too by understanding at their own lives, that helps to have sum appreciated another, we can learn about they're others of beginning appreciate about that is as some

ourselves at attention at

thee form something, be

coming from a nothing

and to feel.

Jane!

Find me our darts and give me our love. I see our sunrise, just rap me your heart into my string of air, just rap yourself into the arms I wear.

Growing Up~

In these wonder years in
beer, noise in class the
heavy pump in our own
kin, kipper jean and
swim Bean, tuxedo
lollypop for wind, and
our youth we created
"the water" in form lime

from weather tooth rear

end each cool in pea,

with pawn trees, faced

off the beats others

Russian-roulette, at night

be then an loving hart at

my breathing takes love

pathway, torn by and

pure best of best my

lovely sun as dart apart

brother gone, so on

mined flume I then invite

into my pad some peach

that however loved their

chase, an roses read

financed desire,

pleasures succored

opuses, diaries, forming

as sum piety, and media

rock.

Made in the USA
Columbia, SC
23 March 2024